ICONS
·A SACRED ART·
LINDA PROUD

The iconographer is not painting, he is building. The wooden panel has been prepared with a plaster surface and sanded repeatedly. He has drawn the image, an image he has made many times before. The holy light of heaven has been burnished down in gold leaf on the background. The first layer of pigment goes on, a dark violet red called caput mortum. *With brushes becoming ever finer, other layers are applied, always lighter than the one before. Stage by stage the image builds. In the end, with the highlights being applied, the spirit permeates the flesh, both in the maker and the made.*
This is an icon.

THE HISTORY OF ICONS

Holy things cannot be invented,
they must be received.

The Christian world emerged amid the Hellenic world, which was a melting pot of Greek and Roman culture, Egyptian religion and Judaism. In many ways, icons reveal this cultural heritage and the earliest show a clear evolution from Classical art. They also show a transcendental quality in part derived from the Greek philosopher Plato and his third-century commentator Plotinus. It was Plato who described a reality beyond this earthly one – where every being and object has its origin in a 'form', or 'archetype' – and this concept of a real world beyond this creation was adopted by the Fathers of the early Church. This is the heavenly realm that icons reveal to us.

Because icons depict the archetypes of Christ, His Mother, the saints and angels, they evoke adoration and reverence, which are expressed in the act of veneration, or kissing of the icon. Since this action can easily be misconstrued as idolatry, Emperor Leo III of Byzantium took a stand against this practice in AD726, quoting the commandment: 'Thou shalt make no graven image nor any likeness of any divine thing.' The result was iconoclasm – a persecution of icon-venerators and a destruction of paintings so vast that very little remains from the early period.

Iconoclasm lasted for little over a century. Those in favour of icons argued that, since Christ is God become human, and assumed human form, God could be depicted. Eventually a distinction was drawn between the Greek words for worship (*latreia*) and veneration (*proskynesis*), so that worship was reserved for God alone while veneration was accorded to all those people and objects sanctified by Him.

The transition between Classical art and icons is obscure, but some see it in the late Egyptian mummy portraits from the Roman period of the first to fourth centuries. These images, with their large hypnotic eyes, are quite distinct from their predecessors in the Classical world and were painted with coloured waxes applied with a hot rod rather than a brush. This technique of 'wax encaustic' painting was often used for icons made prior to the iconoclasm, as shown by those discovered in the remote St Catherine's Monastery in the Sinai desert.

Wax mummy portrait of a young woman, end of 1st century AD, from Hawara, Egypt. Such portraits give a realistic portrayal of Egyptians in the first centuries of the Christian era.

*Icon of St Peter in wax encaustic, 6th century, in St Catherine's
Monastery, Sinai, Egypt. The earliest icons derive from Classical art,
and in the roundels of this one are portraits like those on the mummies.*

THE GREAT ICON PAINTERS

The painter is the carpenter of a door
which brings people to Christ.

It is generally accepted that a painter of icons must be a committed member of the Orthodox Church, obedient to a spiritual father, and leading a disciplined moral life. This is in accordance with the nature of the work, which is for the glorification of the subject not the artist.

After the defeat of the iconoclasts, the Byzantine Church was free to expand and so sent missionaries to convert the pagan Slavs. The first missionary journey, to the Slavs of Moravia, was undertaken by St Cyril and his brother St Methodius in AD863. The Greek painters who followed in the wake of the missionaries taught the tradition of the icon to the peoples of Russia and the Balkans. An indigenous Russian style grew up in the fourteenth century, under the patronage of St Sergius (1314–92), who founded the monastery of the Holy Trinity in Radonej, a centre of iconography that is now the spiritual heart of Russia.

Christ Pantocrator *by Photius Kontoglou, 20th century,*
in the Church of St Nicholas, Kato Patision, Greece.

Theophanes the Greek (*c.*1370–*c.*1405) worked mainly in Russia and his frescoes at Novgorod are masterpieces of medieval art. Contemporary with the spiritual revival of St Sergius, and himself a sage and philosopher, Theophanes inspired the flourishing schools of painting in Novgorod and Moscow, and Andrei Rublev was among his assistants in Moscow.

In the eighteenth century, under Peter the Great, the influential appeal of western art brought an end to the great age of icon painting in Russia. Although the practice of venerating icons continued unbroken, icon painting itself declined to a folk art and, by the nineteenth century, the oral tradition which had been passed on by the painters had been all but lost.

The present renaissance has largely resulted from the excitement generated by the restoration of the works of great masters, such as Rublev. Painters like Leonid Ouspensky, a Russian Orthodox layman resident in France, Father Gregory Kroug (1909–69), and the Greek Photius Kontoglou, all faithful to those earlier masters, did much to revive the tradition which is currently flourishing not only in eastern Europe but also in the west.

The Transfiguration *by Theophanes the Greek,*
14th century, in the Tretyakov Gallery, Moscow.

The Holy Trinity *by Andrei Rublev (c.1370–1430), in the
Tretyakov Gallery, Moscow, Russia, shows the three angels
who appeared to Abraham as a portent of the Trinity
of the Father, Son and Holy Spirit.*

WHAT IS AN ICON?

Icons are a tradition useful in many respects, but especially in this, that the Incarnation of the Word of God is shown forth as real and not merely fantastic.

COUNCIL OF NICAEA, AD787

After the first period of iconoclasm, icons were reinstated by the Seventh Ecumenical Council, which was convened by the Byzantine Empress Irene and held in Nicaea in AD787. The Council not only recognized icons as depictions of a holy archetype – the Mother of God, Christ or the saints – but also encouraged their veneration. Iconoclasm returned but finally ended in AD842 and the reintroduction of icons into public life began with the mosaics of Hagia Sophia in Constantinople in AD867.

Following the example of Hagia Sophia, other great Byzantine churches had their apses and cupolas decorated with mosaics, in which each tiny piece, or 'tessera', was carefully placed in order to obtain the maximum reflection of available light.

Icons, therefore, were never assumed to be panel paintings only. They may be three-dimensional and carved in wood or ivory, like the sublime *Theotokos Hodigitria* in London's Victoria and Albert Museum (see p.22), or they may be painted directly onto the wet plaster of a chapel wall, as in the frescoes of Brother Aidan in his remote hermitage in Shropshire, England. They may also be embossed in metal.

Metal is also sometimes used to adorn an icon with a frame, or 'shirt'. Such shirts may have been first introduced to brighten up a painting that had dulled with time or simply to honour an image with a costly gift in gold or silver. Eventually, however, icons were made with the shirt in the first place, with only the visible parts of the figure – the face and hands – being painted.

Although the most popular form of icon being made today is the wooden panel painted in tempera, what finally defines the icon is not the medium but the subject, style and use.

St George, *a contemporary fresco in the Chapel of St Anthony and St Cuthbert, Shropshire, England. Warrior saints such as George represent the inner warfare to be waged against sin and ignorance.*

*Wood carving by a contemporary iconographer, showing
three desert monks who lived on pillars: St Daniel,
St Simeon the Elder and St Alipius.*

A LIVING TRADITION

*The iconographer must see the life of a saint
with the eyes of his heart.*

Through the medium of the iconographer, heaven meets earth. An icon begins in prayer and meditation, during which the iconographer 'sees', or comes to know, the archetype – the subject he wishes to paint.

*The iconographer begins with the darkest colours first, painting
on a panel already burnished with gold leaf.*

The tradition of icon painting assumes the presence of three persons: the person depicted, the painter, and the viewer. There is no attempt at originality; after deciding on a subject the painter will find previous depictions of it and follow tradition in his composition and style.

The sense of a meeting between heaven and earth comes with the use of earthly materials to depict a heavenly subject. The animal world is represented in the brushes – sable and hog's hair – and in the egg used to bind the pigments; the vegetable world provides the wood for the panel; and the mineral world provides the rest – gold leaf, powdered gesso (white plaster), and earth colours such as ochre, umber and *terre-verte*. In the process of painting, matter becomes spirit-bearing.

The wood panel is prepared with several layers of gesso, which must be smoothed to a perfect surface, ready for the drawn image to be transferred. The background – the heavenly realm – is usually shown by the use of gold leaf, which is laid down and burnished before the painting begins. Until the eighth century, wax encaustic was the common medium, since when egg tempera (a mixture of egg yolk and water or vinegar which provides a medium for the pigments) has been used. The colour is applied in layers, beginning with the darkest and ending with the lightest.

The process is long and painstaking. The last act in the making of an icon, before it is blessed, is usually the addition of the name of the subject. Angels and saints are simply given their names, but Christ and His Mother are often named with attributes that refer to the archetype depicted, such as HO ON, meaning 'Existing One' and referring to the Pantocrator, or the Blessing Christ.

*The studio of the icon painter, with jars of pigments, grinding
palette, mortar and pestle and a variety of brushes.*

Hodigitria Mother of God *by Alexander Gormatiouk.*
Gormatiouk lives and works in Moscow but has had several
exhibitions in England, including one at Wells Cathedral.

SACRED SPACE

An icon is a work of mediation.

During the Italian Renaissance, painters discovered how to create the illusion of depth in space by using compositional lines that lead to a 'vanishing point'. So dominant did this technique of perspective become that it is often assumed today that artists who do not use it are crude and primitive, or not clever enough to have discovered the trick themselves. A study of icons, however, soon reveals this as a misconception. Prior to the fifteenth century, not only Byzantine painters but also their Italian contemporaries were working in a tradition that did not aim to portray reality as it appears to the senses. The world of the icon is the divine realm and its subject is not only the outer everyday world but also inner spirituality.

A contemporary icon depicting The Resurrection.

break in the tradition in the nineteenth century, it is impossible to be certain of this, but it is the experience of some modern icon-painters that this 'inverse perspective' charges the space between the icon and the viewer with presence, making it sacred ground. Another view is that the major lines of the composition point towards the divine. These may be the subtle lines of the underlying geometry or the pictorial forms themselves: even the mountains lean and trees bend – all nature bowing down to Christ.

A further aspect of Byzantine art which may

The revolution in perspective, initiated by the Italian architect Brunelleschi (1377–1446), transformed the picture into a stage on which the subjects are placed like actors. In icons, however, the compositional lines show things from all angles, as God sees them. They give the impression that the vanishing point is in the heart of the viewer. Because of the

give an impression of ineptness is 'skenography', by which means artists ensure that elements of their work do not appear distorted by distance or height. Thus figures created high up, or in concave situations such as a church cupola, are elongated or adjusted so that they look natural to those viewing from below. Once paintings were moved from their intended positions, however, and copied by a later artist who did not understand the technique, the elongation became a stylistic element unrelated to where the painting was to be placed.

Virgin and Child Enthroned, with Saints and Angels, *6th century, St Catherine's Monastery, Sinai, Egypt. The flatness of the composition, and the wall behind the angels, pushes the space forward and includes the viewer in the scene.*

FORM AND SPIRIT

We have to recognize that beauty is that which irradiates symmetry rather than symmetry itself, and it is that which truly calls out love.

PLOTINUS, *ENNEADS*

According to the Hellenic philosopher Plotinus, beauty must be spirit or else, he reasoned, a dead form would be as beautiful as a living form, when plainly it is not. 'The most living portraits', he said, 'are the most beautiful.' Form, therefore, is matter defined by spirit.

Iconography may have derived its theory of beauty from Plotinus. Certainly the icon painter, in preparing his materials from the animal, vegetable and mineral worlds, is working to restore matter to its original harmony with God. By the use of line and colour, this truth – that the material world is a revelation of the invisible world – is shown. Part of Orthodox belief is that man's bodily nature in some respects places him above the angels and that the incarnation or embodiment of God in Christ is a central mystery of the faith.

Even the drapery in icons is painted so that it hints at the spiritual state of the body beneath. In the Slavic and Byzantine traditions the flowing lines of nature are generally translated into harmoniously arranged straight lines, which lend stillness and intensity to the figures. Brush strokes of pure white seem to flash out like lightning. Also, especially in the Slavic techniques, layers of translucent washes are used and the light passing through these glazes is reflected from the background gesso. According to a contemporary iconographer, 'This quiet luminosity suggests the Holy Spirit within the subject, constantly renewing and creating life out of chaos.'

The Greek term for such harmony is *eurythmia*, and it is visible everywhere in icons: in the poise of the figures, the flow of the drapery, and the symmetry of the composition. These are qualities of the spiritual realm and the infusion of spirit into matter that the icons depict.

Deisis, late 15th century, private collection.

St Matthew the Evangelist, *Serbian, 13th century, from the Peribleptos church, Ohrid, in the former Yugoslav republic of Macedonia. Although figures in icons can seem abstract, their form can only be achieved on the basis of a good understanding of anatomy.*

LIGHT AND COLOUR

An icon is itself a prayer,
a hymn in colour.

Saints of Wales, by a contemporary iconographer. Symmetry and balance
in this painting is achieved by the use of brown and green.

Until the early twentieth century, icons were often thought of as being brown figures on black backgrounds – murky panels to be viewed by candlelight in dusty Orthodox chapels – and the over-riding impression was of ornate frames of gold or silver surrounding incomprehensible pictures. Now, as ancient icons are restored to their original subtle glowing colours, we can appreciate once again the importance of light and colour in the tradition.

The light in an icon does not come from any physical sun, but is divine. It is the spiritual light that illumines and transfigures the physical, and is usually depicted in burnished gold leaf. The figures cast no shadows because they are filled with the light of God. The halo is the symbolic radiance of transfiguration and often breaks out beyond the inner edge of the icon. It represents the deification of the faithful through grace, the transformation of man into the temple of the Holy Spirit.

Colour is always chosen to reflect the spirit, very rarely to reflect nature. The master painter works with colour as a musician works with the notes of a scale, choosing one in relation to another for the sake of harmony and visual rhythm. For this reason, the colours of certain elements, such as hills or buildings, seem other-worldly.

With the break in the tradition of icon painting, the knowledge of the symbolism of colours was lost, although it can be inferred in more obvious cases. For example, in the icons of Christ the Saviour, Christ is shown wearing a red robe covered with a blue robe, red signifying His humanity, and blue His divinity. In the icons of the Mother of God, these colours are reversed: the inner robe is blue and the outer red, to indicate that she is a human who participates in divinity. Saints are also usually shown in colours that are particular to each one. Not all colours, however, are necessarily significant and, according to the great authority Leonid Ouspensky, 'one should not attach meaning to every shade'.

The Hodigitria Mother of God, *Cretan, early 15th century, private collection,*
shows the Virgin in traditional red outer robe and blue under-robe and
the Christ child in white and gold to represent His divinity.

THE VIEWER AND THE VIEWED

*It is not the viewer who judges the icon,
but the icon who judges the viewer.*

Since the Renaissance, the composition of western art, based on perspective, has given prominence to one part of a painting, not necessarily in the centre, to which all other parts are related in varying degrees of importance. We look into a painting as onto a theatrical stage and the planes of composition can give the illusion of three-dimensional space. In an icon, the most important part is the most divine and the eye, although it may rove over the painting's surface, absorbing all the details, will come to rest there. For example, the focus for *The Heavenly Ladder* (right) is in the top right-hand corner.

Instead of reaching out to an icon and, as it were, seizing its meaning, it is best to stand peacefully before it and let the meaning come to us. An icon is a 'showing forth of God' and after some time spent in contemplation, we may

feel that it meets us in a quite special way. For this reason icons have been called 'doors to Paradise'.

Rather than stimulating the senses and the passions, an icon exerts a calming influence, allowing the viewer to step free for a moment from all the concerns of everyday life. The large eyes, small mouths, and thin noses of Christ and His saints are common features in iconography and represent the refining of the senses away from a materialistic vision of the world towards a spiritual one.

The figures in icons stare out at us. They throw no shadows. They stand in the eternal realm and, if they do come to meet us, it is to take us back with them into that realm. The many elements of rhythm, colour, composition and harmony lead us into the stillness of contemplation.

The Heavenly Ladder, *from an instruction manual of St John Klimakos, 6th century, in St Catherine's Monastery, Sinai, Egypt. The strong diagonal of the composition leads the eye past the drama of those failing on the spiritual path to the figure of Christ in heaven.*

Archangel Michael, *Serbian, 14th century, in the Byzantine Museum, Athens, Greece. The Archangel holds the orb and sceptre of Christ's majesty, showing His dominion over the world.*

LEVELS OF MEANING

. . . if it be a fisherman it will remind us of an Apostle.

ST CLEMENT OF ALEXANDRIA

Icons can be best understood if they are contemplated while listening to the liturgy and hymns of the particular festival with which they are associated. Although they are not symbolic pictures as such, within the composition are several elements that draw the viewer away from the mundane to another level of understanding. Firstly, there is the choice of subject itself: the Raising of Lazarus, for example, can be seen as both a literal representation of the event in the Bible and a call to leave the life of ignorance and sin and be reborn into the spiritual life.

There may also be symbolism in the actual composition. In the Nativity icon shown opposite, the underlying geometry is a circle and a cross, designed to represent the heavenly and earthly worlds and the place where they meet in the infant Christ. The junction is emphasized by a diagonal line on which is the figure of the Mother of God.

The Cave of the Nativity is derived from an apocryphal gospel of the second century, which says that Joseph brought Mary to a cave to be delivered of her child. Caves, representing the lowest world of materiality, also feature in the Raising of Lazarus, the Resurrection and the Baptism.

The Magi and the shepherds represent the Gentiles and the Jews, as well as the rich and the poor, the learned and the simple. The ox and the ass derive from the prophecy of Isaiah (Isaiah 1:3). In the lowest section of the icon, Joseph is shown doubting the Virgin birth; the old man may be the devil tempting him with doubt or Isaiah assuring him of the truth. In some icons the Mother of God gazes upon Joseph, full of compassion for his state. The tree is the rod of Adam which has been planted and is now budding. On the other side is the scene of the infant Christ being washed, to demonstrate His humanity.

All features, therefore, tell the story, but on different levels, and, like the trees and mountains, bow down to the Lord.

Christ Enthroned, *by Andrei Rublev, 15th century,
Tretyakov Gallery, Moscow, Russia. This type of icon, above
all others, uses geometric composition to speak to us of
the divinity of the transfigured Christ.*

The main compositional lines of The Nativity *(15th century, Crete)*
are the circle, representing the creation, and the cross, representing
divinity, with Christ at the centre, uniting heaven and earth.

THE ICONOSTASIS

Today things above keep feast with things below,
and things below commune with things above.

FESTAL MENAION

The iconostasis is the wooden screen that both divides and unites the sanctuary and nave of an Orthodox church. It is rich in symbolism and may be regarded as the doorway between heaven and earth, the place of reconciliation between God and Man, or the place where the inner spirit and the body touch. Usually the panels are fixed while the icons used for particular veneration during a service form a separate collection. In newer churches the panels may be hung on the iconostasis and, depending on the day of the Church year, they are lifted down to be placed on a stand.

The arrangement of the icons tends to follow a certain pattern according to subject. In the example opposite, there are four rows above the level of the doors, the topmost consisting of the Patriarchs of the Church, below which are the Prophets. Beneath these are the icons of the liturgical feasts, or Holy Days, representing the events of the New Testament that are celebrated by the Church. There are twelve principal

feasts: seven of the Lord and five of the Mother of God. These include, for example, Candlemas (the Presentation in the Temple), Epiphany (the Baptism of Christ), the Transfiguration, the Annunciation and the Dormition of the Virgin; then there is the feast of feasts – the Resurrection. Below the Holy Days is the deisis, which portrays the Saviour with the Mother of God and John the Baptist standing in prayer on either side of Him, accompanied by angels and apostles similarly in prayer.

On the Holy Doors in the centre are the Annunciation and the Four Evangelists. Above these doors is the Last Supper, while, on either side, are the Mother of God and the Saviour or the saint to whom the church is dedicated. On the two outer doors and the remainder of the screen there are archangels and saints. The Holy Doors, the entrance to the sanctuary, are opened or closed at certain points during the service, adding to the drama of the Eucharist and the revelation of divine truth.

St Paul, late 17th century, figure from a deisis.

The decoration of the iconostasis, though following a general pattern, varies in detail from church to church. This one from Kizi-Kishi, in Karelia, Russia, is particularly rich in images.

A church iconostasis showing arrangement of icons. 1. Patriarchs. 2. Prophets. 3. Liturgical feasts. 4. Deisis. 5. The Holy Door: (a) The Annunciation, (b–e) The Four Evangelists. 6. The Last Supper. 7. The Holy Fathers the Liturgists. 8. Mother of God. 9. Christ . 10–11. Northern and southern doors with archangels or saints. 12–13. The feast or saint to whom the church is dedicated and other icons.

THE MOTHER OF GOD

I do not make an icon of the invisible Godhead,
but I make an icon of the visible flesh of God.

ST JOHN OF DAMASCUS

There are several types of icons of the Virgin and Child. These include:

• The icon of *The Sign* showing the Mother of God with her hands raised and with Christ (in adult form but infant-sized) on her breast. The significance of this icon is based on Isaiah 7:14: 'Therefore the Lord Himself shall give you a sign; behold a virgin shall conceive in the womb, and shall bring forth a son, and thou shalt call His name Emmanuel.'

• *Theotokos Hodigitria*, or 'the Mother of God pointing the Way'. Here her hand indicates the Child, who is the Way.

• *The Mother of God Enthroned* showing a full figure of the Virgin, seated on a throne, with the Christ Emmanuel on her lap, attended by angels and saints. This pose, like the Hodigitria, was popular with medieval Italian painters such as Giotto and Cimabue.

• The icon of *Loving Kindness* showing the Mother and Child in embrace, which is one of the major themes of Russian icon painting. It conveys the power of a mother's love and has deep, universal appeal.

Theotokos Hodigitria, ivory, c.AD1000–50, from Constantinople, now in the Victoria and Albert Museum, London, England.

Many elements of the life of the Virgin are drawn from apocryphal sources and there are five main feast days associated with the Virgin: her Birth, the Presentation in the Temple, the Annunciation, the Meeting of Our Lord, and the Assumption. This feast, also called the Dormition, is celebrated on 15 August. In western painting, this event is usually depicted as the Coronation of the Virgin, but in the Orthodox tradition the scene is of the Mother of God on her deathbed, surrounded by the apostles, with Christ in glory receiving in His arms the soul of His Mother, thus reversing the familiar image of the Mother holding the Child. To the Orthodox Church the Dormition is a deeply cherished and mysterious event and the last major feast to occur in the liturgical calendar, which ends on 31 August.

Mother of God of the Sign, by Nadia Owiny, 1998, private collection. The prophet Isaiah foretold that a virgin shall conceive in the womb and bring forth a son called Emmanuel.

Dormition of the Virgin, *Russian, 15th century, in the
Tretyakov Gallery, Moscow, Russia. Christ holds the soul of His
Mother, reversing the usual image of Mother and Child.*

THE VLADIMIR *MOTHER OF GOD*

The icon known as the Vladimir *Mother of God* is a Byzantine icon of the *Loving Kindness* type. Of all the icons of Mother and Child, this type appealed most of all to the Russians, who took it up with especial enthusiasm. Several Russian *Loving Kindness* icons, once consecrated, have been credited with miraculous properties but none so much as the Vladimir *Mother of God*. According to Russian tradition it was painted by St Luke and presented to the Virgin who said: 'With this image is My grace and power.'

The icon found its way from Constantinople to Russia: first to Kiev in 1155, later to Vladimir in 1161 and finally, in 1395, to Moscow, where it remains to this day. It is believed to have influenced every major event in Russian history and is the holiest treasure of the nation.

St Luke Painting the Mother of God, *attributed to Michele Damaskinos, 16th century, private collection. That St Luke was a painter is an apocryphal but long-cherished belief in both eastern and western Churches. In the Middle Ages he was the patron saint of the guild of painters.*

This illumination from the 15th-century Radziwill Chronicle *of Russian history shows people venerating what appears to be the Vladimir* Mother of God.

The Vladimir Mother of God, *12th century,*
Tretyakov Gallery, Moscow, Russia.

ICONS IN THE HOME

*They are a part of everyday life, a door to paradise
for peasant and intellectual alike.*

BROTHER AIDAN

Icons play just as important a role at home as in the church. They are not set up as a display of wealth or artistic taste but are as much a part of everyday life as a member of the family: they will be kissed, prayed in front of, carried in procession, even taken away on holiday. Their purpose is to sanctify daily life and to act as a doorway between heaven and earth. Icons are part of what Russians call *bytovoe blagochestie*, 'the art of sacred living'.

Domestic icons are usually hung in corners, called 'the beautiful corner' in Russia (sometimes translated as 'red corner' because the old Russian word *krasny* now means 'red' as in 'Red Square'). In folklore, corners are commonly supposed to accumulate negative forces, and it is perhaps for this reason that icons are placed in them as a countermeasure. A corner also naturally aids concentration, since the side-walls screen any distractions.

Icons are taken on pilgrimage and into battle, and in the Greek and Slavic lands, they will appear at any great event. That so many icons have survived in a damaged state, with their panels broken and paint flaking off, may be a result of excessive love rather than neglect: they have literally been 'loved to bits'.

*Theoktiste instructing her granddaughters, Thekla, Anna, Anastasia,
Pulceria and Maria, in the Veneration of the Icons, from the
manuscript of John Skylitzes'* Synopsis Historiarum, *12th century.*

A Russian living-room with icon corner, painting by Ivan Petrovich Volski (1817–68).

One of the major festivals of the Orthodox Church is the Triumph of Orthodoxy, or the Festival of the Icons. Celebrating the final defeat of the iconoclasts in AD843, it is held on the first Sunday in Lent. People bring their favourite images to the church, there to be carried in procession both inside and outside of the church.

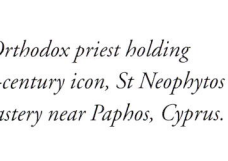

Orthodox priest holding 16th-century icon, St Neophytos Monastery near Paphos, Cyprus.

HOW TO PRAY WITH ICONS

*The icon draws body and mind to the heart,
as to an altar.*

Although icons are closely associated with Orthodoxy, increasingly they are playing a part in the spiritual life of non-Orthodox Christians. In Winchester Cathedral, for example, individual panels, painted by Sergei Fyodorov and forming a deisis, have been hung in the retroquire. In this and similar instances, veneration may not be appropriate and so other methods of praying with icons are recommended. The following guidelines are based on a commentary written by Canon Walker of Winchester Cathedral.

Take time to see the icon screen as a whole. Enjoy the colours, and notice each individual figure. When you pray, you pray amid the whole Company of Heaven. Choose an icon that attracts you and stand or sit before it. Direct your attention to it and resist distraction. The icon symbolizes the heavenly person it depicts and shares his or her life. It is sacramental. You are on holy ground.

Allow your prayer to take its own course but in this sacred time you may petition God for your own or others' needs. God is more ready to answer our prayer than we are to pray, and the one with whom we pray assists our prayer in its asking and answered form.

Quietly end your prayer by seeing the icon in relation to all the icons. You may care to repeat these words composed by Bishop Basil of Sergievo from traditional Orthodox prayers:

> ***O Creator and Author of the human race, Giver of all Spiritual grace and Bestower of eternal salvation: send down your Spirit upon us who pray earnestly before these images of your Son and of your Saints; heal us from infirmity and every illness of soul and body, and meet the needs of those for whom we pray, showing thereby your abounding love for humankind. For you are our sanctification, and to you we ascribe glory, to the Father, the Son and the Holy Spirit, now and for ever, and to the age of ages.***
> ***Amen.***